MOON JOURNAL

transform

BY

Katie Jo

Moon Journal Transform
Copyright © 2021 by Katie Jo Finai

All rights reserved. No part of this publication may be reproduced, stored in a retrieval system, or transmitted in any for or by any means, electronic, mechanical, photocopying, recording, or otherwise, without written permission of the publisher or author, except for the use of brief quotations in a book review.

Although the author and publisher have made every effort to ensure that the information in this book was correct at press time, the author and publisher do not assume and hereby disclaim any liability to any party for any loss, damage, or disruption caused by errors or omissions, whether such errors or omissions result from negligence, accident, or any other cause.

Adherence to all applicable laws and regulations, including international, federal, state and local governing professional licensing, business practices, advertising, and all other aspects of doing business in the US, Canada or any other jurisdiction is the sole responsibility of the reader and consumer.

Neither the author nor the publisher assumes any responsibility or liability whatsoever on behalf of the consumer or reader of this material. Any per¬ceived slight of any individual or organization is purely unintentional.

The resources in this book are provided for informational purposes only and should not be used to replace the specialized training and professional judgment of a health care or mental health care professional.

Neither the author nor the publisher can be held responsible for the use of the information provided within this book. Please always consult a trained professional before making any decision regarding treatment of yourself or others.

To request permissions, contact the publisher at
freedomhousepublishingco@gmail.com or katiejosoul@gmail.com

Paperback ISBN: 978-1-952566-22-6
Printed in the USA.
Freedom House Publishing Co
Middleton, ID 83644
www.freedomhousepublishingco.com

Since the beginning of time, all animals on the planet have lived in harmony with the natural cycles and flow of the seasons, moons, and magnetic pull of the planetary system. This intuitive knowledge is within our very DNA, we are programmed to live in the FLOW and song of the universe.

However, in modern day- we have separated ourselves from these cycles with technology and industry. Indeed, while all other mammals on the planet are resting and rejuvenating in the winter; humans are working the same as we do all summer. Instead of waking with the sun and resting with its sunset- we use synthetic systems like alarm clocks and cell phones to tell us when our body sleeps and wakes.

Modern technology is amazing. It has done wonders for the human race; but it has also served to disconnect us from the patterns and intuitions of nature that are inherent to our biological system. This Moon Journal is meant to support you in reharmonizing and re-integrating the natural rhythms into your life.

The moon has held mystery and magic from the beginning of all time. Indeed, the story of the Earth as we know it- doesn't speak without the Moon also.

The moon has represented many things to many cultures and belief and esoteric and modern-day ceremonies. It has been worshipped, revered, and feared throughout time and as the wheel of history has turned; the meaning behind the moon has changed and shifted- just like the everchanging face of light that it reflects.

In our day and age, we are emerging from the scientific blinding of all energetic and ideological theory- only to have science conclude that there are energetic phenomena that cannot be logically quantified. And, in scientific and medical fields; the effect of the moon in its phase has been proven to make a difference geologically, astrologically, energetically, and medically.

The moon creates the ocean tides, lifts the soil, and affects planting of crops and growth of seeds. In emergency rooms, medical staff is increased to plan on more inflow of patients. The moon not only pulls on the ocean, water, and dirt- it pulls on the blood in our bodies, and earth elements we are made of.

We ARE Earth and Water. The moon affects us. We are Nature. The moon is part of OUR system, our flow, our energetic and physical experience. Learning to "flow" with the ebbs and rise of the moon energy, being conscious of it and in partnership with it; can dramatically change your life.

Instead of "fighting" what energies are around us; by making simple and subtle shifts to our way of living and being; we harmoniously move into peace and understanding of ourselves.

As we live within the natural rhythms of natures; life becomes the symphony; a dance. Katie Jo

How to use this journal:

**This Workbook is meant for YOU
to be the guide of your own journey.**

**I have outlined meanings of the moon
cycles, and astrological events
over the next year for you
to interpret as you choose.**

**The Moons are listed in order of
occurrence, starting with the
WOLF MOON in January and its essence.
But decide for yourself what
that moon means to you.**

**Follow in order or don't.
There are promptings for writings
and journaling throughout the year.**

---

*If you didn't believe in the power
of the moon at all,
this journal could change
your life by simply
setting new goals
and releasing old
habits and thought patterns
13 times a year.
(Moon Cycles)*

Contents

The First part of this journal explains the basics of the Moon meanings and other significant celestial occurrences.

The cycle of moons are listed in order, as well as promptings to assist you in using the moon energy to set intentions and goals and address the areas of your life, while following the natural flow of the seasons.

There are suggested processes for full and new moon, and other areas of your life, as well as dream work ideas.

The Final Pages are for you to journal and make notes, use the promptings or come up with your own.

This next year of moons can be the greatest of your life.

It's up to you.

The moon phases made simple: Full Moon gets a lot of attention, but New Moon is the balance of Full moon, and equally important and potent.

Full Moon Basics:
This is the time of
GRATITUDE.
Full Moon=Full Heart. BE Grateful, acknowledge the abundance and expansion and bounty in your life and relationships. FULL MOON also begins the releasing cycle. As the light reflected across its face begins to diminish- it energetically supports us RELEASING whatever we would like to let go of.

New Moon Basics:
This is a time of
CREATION.
New Moon=
New Beginnings
New Moon is the growth of light and expansion. It is the time to set new goals and make new plans. To plant seeds and set intentions. As the light grows over the next few weeks; it supports the expansion and growth of the New Beginnings.

FULL MOON Mantra: I am grateful for the LIGHT in my life. I am LIGHT. I am FREE. I am a reflection of all Light and I am Light within. I release any and all illusions that I have created or believed that inhibit my knowing of this truth. I release any and all blocks to my perfect prosperity, Love Relationship, abundance and health. I release any subconscious programming that I am aware or unaware of that is delaying my ascension and manifestation of knowing my perfect light and LOVING myself as is.

NEW MOON Mantra:

I am grateful. I am free. I create, manifest, and easily receive the prosperity, guidance, intuition, and grace that I am born worthy of. I am infinite. I am Free. I am one with all and I am all in one. I easily create and manifest the light I choose, the love I choose, the finances I choose, the destiny I choose. I Am that I Am.

Water Ceremonies for Moon:

The moon is intrinsically linked to the water. The gravitational pull of the water creates the ocean tides, lifts soil, and magnetizes iron infused rock. (Red Rock)

Full moon is the time for Bathing, Bubble Baths, Drinking Moon Water, eliminating alcohol or other toxins that contaminate your blood. Drink clear healthy water.

Water is the element of Emotion.

Often, we are like the waves of the Ocean- reactive to all the storms around us. Influenced by the people, situations and experiences around us. The waves are powerful- yes... but the greatest power is the deep, never ending Ocean beneath. This is representative of our subconscious and depth. When we are in peace and balance with our emotions- we are like the Ocean water untouched by the turmoil of the world.

The deep Ocean is connected to ALL the water in the world, in the FLOW of water life cycle, the raindrops that touch the sky; the rainstorms that water the mountain tops, nourish the plants and soil- to return back to their home; the Ocean.

Meditation is about going to the deep places. Unafraid.
To meditate, create a bath or pour a glass of water into a beautiful goblet.
Breathe deeply from your abdomen and
 imagine that the water in you and the water
in the bath or goblet are ONE. Visualize
the journey this water has taken. Starting
with the evaporation into mist and sky,
until dense and heavy enough to return to
Earth. Dew on grass or leaves, soaking into
 the musky Earth, being drawn by gravity to
the rivers; and eventually- into the bosom of the Ocean.

Here, the water can be a wave, a droplet, bubbly seafoam, exploring the depths of the sea or glistening in sunlight… until it evaporates again.

Water carries information. We are water. ALL water has existed since the beginning of our planet. WE began in the water, as WE genetically evolved to land animals- we forgot we were and ARE water. All the lifetimes we have lived, all the memories of the ages of time, are held within the water. As we ARE water… the mysteries of the universe and wisdom of our ancestors is inside us. We simply have to unlock them and drink the knowledge.

To create Moon water, you'll need:

A jar or container. Glass is best. Mason Jars work great.

Water (make sure it's safe to drink if you plan on doing so).

Paper and pencil/marker.

Water-safe crystals, like rose quartz, clear quartz, or amethyst (optional).

An intention to focus on, Gratitude and release during FULL MOON, New goals and beginnings during NEW MOON.

Add water to your jar and crystals of your choice.

Use a marker to write a word or blessing on the jar, include the date and Full or New Moon details.

Place your jar somewhere outside, or in a windowsill exposed to the moon light, so it can absorb the Moon's energy—even if you can't see the Moon, the water will still charge.

If you'd like, you can take a moment to meditate: Hold your palms over the water and picture the lunar energy moving through the crown of your head, down your spine and arms, through your body, and out of your palms into the water.

As you do so, focus on the intention you're setting, you can write a prayer or intention on a note and place beneath the jar; "LOVE and GRATITUDE" are considered the most purifying and energizing words.

Finally, leave the water to charge overnight. It is recommended that you retrieve the water before sunlight touches it (solarizes).

Moon Water Uses: Use it to clean your altar, sacred space, crystals, or any ritual tools• Add it to a ritual bath• Use it to cleanse your home• Dip your brushes in it when you paint• Use it to water your plants• Create a fragrant room spray by adding essential oils and alcohol• Use it in your essential oil diffuser• Drink it so you can absorb it into your body• Use it to anoint your body, as a way of energetically cleansing yourself

MOON BATH TEA by Katie Jo:

Create and use as often as you like.

INGREDIENTS
- 1 cup oat flour (you can blend dry oats in your blender)
- 1/4 cup dried lavender buds (called the Mother plant for skin and emotional balance)
- Clary Sage Essential Oil 2/3 drops (opens 3rd eye and soothes emotions)
- Glass jar to store your finished tea, Mason Jars are great! (reuse recycle!)
- Amethyst Crystal (opens intuition, heals, and supports addiction release)
- 1 Cup Epsom Salt (Cleansing and detoxifying)
- Old sock… REALLY.

INSTRUCTIONS
1. In Glass Jar, blend all of your ingredients together (except your crystal) easy to Shake!!
2. Place crystal in jar and set in Moonlight. ANY night works, but FULL MOON is especially potent. If you choose NEW MOON that's a great time for new intentions!
3. Fill a bath with hot water, using a spoon, scoop contents into the sock (crystal is ok) and tie off with twine or make a knot, place sock into water to steep for a minute.
4. Light some candles, meditate, or listen to instrumental music and be open to what the Moon Bath Tea opens your awareness to.
5. Once complete with your experience, you may want to journal or rest. You can reuse the sock once clean, emptying out in nature or dispose in garbage.

Notes

Fire Ceremony:
Fire ceremonies are used for differing reasons. Release is the primary purpose for most ceremonies. In some Shaman cultures, it is taught that when something is set on fire- it is releasing the accumulated LIGHT it has received from its lifetime (often sunlight) and returning it to source.

Basic Fire Ceremony:
Light a candle or campfire, fire pit if available.
Connect to the source within you through breathing slowly; this will regulate your heart rate and release chemicals in your brain that support peace and calmness. Take a sheet of paper and write anything you wish to let go of emotionally, physically, energetically. Write experiences, or relationship dynamics, addictions, memories, grudges, write about subconscious blocks that may be inhibiting you from your dreams. If you don't have the words, then draw or scribble. Fold the paper (as many times as you choose) and with every fold; imagine the issues written getting smaller and smaller and smaller, compressing, becoming insignificant as you recognize you are the master folder, the writer and ultimately the one with the power over these written words and thoughts.

Hold the paper in your hands and speak: **"I release you. I release me. We are light. I am light. May all darkness become light. May all darkness become light. May all darkness become light."**
Burn the paper and watch as it explodes into LIGHT and the smoke carries away to the cosmos. Returned back to sender.
Offer gratitude and blow out the candle or put out the fire completely.

(If you choose, once the fire is cool and safe. You can gather the Ashes of the fire and spread them on sacred land as an offering of gratitude and awareness that it is complete.)

Blue Moon: Blue Moon is when there are two full moons within the same month. This is a DOUBLE whammy of the energy of the Moon Cycle that is occurring. For example: October 2020 was a Full Harvest Moon and BLUE Harvest Moon. Harvest Moon is a time for receiving. It is a time to end a cycle to celebrate your achievements for the year and to take inventory of where you are.

That BLUE Moon was a second energetic opportunity to immerse into the flow. Blue Moons are rare and with them, they bring an added element of magick and mystery.

Lunar Eclipse:

A lunar eclipse is when the shadow of the Earth passes over the moon. These eclipses are times when our subconscious emotions are given a reset. Lunar eclipses are an opportunity for healing and change, to shift the emotional ties that bind us to unforgiveness or subconscious patterns that keep us replaying cycles of sabotage.

The energy of eclipses typically will stay in motion for three months after the eclipse. Often these are powerful events that assist us in "seeing" what our conscious mind was blind to.

By resetting and awakening, these eclipses support us in our overall ascension. We are here on this planet and dimension to return to the knowing of our Divinity. We have forgotten- in order to remember.

Lunar Eclipse Dates and Notes

How am I allowing my emotions and subconscious patterns to affect my life?

What do I choose now?

Solar Eclipse:

A solar eclipse occurs when the moon passes between the Earth and Sun.

The Sun represents focus and in many ways our material world. The moon representing our emotions and subconscious.

These eclipses are pivotal times of change. This offers the opportunity to RESET our focus and attention, our priorities and life path.

As our subconscious pauses; we have the chance to ask ourselves if what we are pursuing or giving our attention to is what we REALLY want.

This is a time to reset our focus and check in with our emotional center. Change the direction or destination of our intentions.

Solar Eclipse Dates and Notes

How does my life reflect my priorities?

Is it time to shift where I'm giving my energy?

Spring Equinox:
Spring Equinox occurs every year when there is equal light and dark

in a 24 hour of time. Moving out of the darker winter months, the universal annual rotation of the planets and Earth in reference to the Sun; the Spring Equinox is the turning point of the year when there will now be MORE sunlight increasing per day until the Summer Solstice. Spring Equinox energy is at its simplest: BALANCE. This is the time of light dawning, seeds in the Earth beginning to awaken and stretch and grow, life is increasing and new realities, new crops, new beginnings are stirring, and it starts with balance.

Balance is beyond light and shadow- but in all areas of our life: Spirit, Mind, Body. This Equinox is a time to start life fresh and new, to BEGIN the CULTIVATION of our dreams. To revitalize our own life, passions, and creativity.

March

Fall Equinox:

Fall Equinox is the time of BALANCE. Equal light and shadow as we move into the Darker months of the year. The winter months are a time of the cocoon. The time to go within and to rest physically but make inner work the focus. Fall Equinox is the time of Gratitude and acknowledging and receiving. Just like the harvest of the work we have done all year, it is now time to see the balance of your life, relationships, dreams and goals. Taking inventory without judgement or lack, but integrity. As the winter months progress, rest, rejuvenate. Learn from nature that sleeps and slumbers. The pinecones and seeds have fallen into the earth and wait to expand until the time and circumstances are right. Winter is the time for INNER WORK. Reading, writing, learning. Preparing the soil for the light. Readying to be successful and thriving. Nourish your mind, body, and spirit during this time. Study what you have been neglecting, self-care and nurture your relationships and dreams.

Summer Solstice:

Summer Solstice is June 21-22. The day when we have more sunlight than any other day of the year. It is the CRESCENDO of LIGHT. This is a day to REVEL in, do CEREMONY in, RECEIVE and IMMERSE yourself in LIGHT. We are LIGHT. This is a time for gratitude and joy and abundance. SEE the great and marvelous things, acknowledge the magick and beauty of being alive. Rise with Sunlight and watch the Sunset. Gather with others to celebrate and do ceremony embodying and embracing the light.

Summer Solstice Notes

What are the greatest reminders of Light in my Life?

How am I living my Light?

Winter Solstice:

Winter Solstice is December 21-22. This is the darkest day of the year. At the top of the world, the sun dips beneath the horizon and there is no light. Winter Solstice is the subconscious. This is a time to feel and be intuitive. During this time, the darkness is reminiscent of the journey to this 3rd dimension. We have left the light, and in the darkness, we must find the LIGHT within ourselves- to lead from our own inner knowing and guidance. This is a reminder to us all that the LIGHT is not outside of us; but within us. That in the darkest hour- we ARE the LIGHT and when the outside world does not "provide" us with light- to BE IT. This is powerful day for ceremony and fire ceremonies. To declare and redefine the LIGHT you know yourself to be and the LIGHT you bring. What LIGHT would you see in the World? What LIGHT do you acknowledge?

BE THE LIGHT.

Winter Solstice Notes

What Light am I?

What Light do I bring to the world?

Who am I really - as a Divine Soul?

What are my unique gifts and talents?

Relationship Process:

The Full Moon is an energetically packed time emotionally.
Often, leading up to Full Moon, couples can feel the pressure of their emotions bubbling up.
This is a time to speak your truths with compassion.
Remember to be grateful and make a list about what you love about your partner.
This is also a time to evaluate your boundaries.
Partners, often Show us where we still have growth to occur.

Take time to be together in sensual and nourishing ways.

Be together without distractions.
Rub lotion on each other's feet.

Say words of encouragement.

Have great sex.

How my Partner Balances me.

RELATIONSHIP

New Moon

What I create in my perfect LOVE relationship: I ask and receive what I am willing to give.

What does your dream relationship look like?
Write the way it feels, the way you treat one another, the life you choose, the lifestyle you have, the kindness you share, the dreams you pursue together.
Remember, whatever you ask for, be willing to give.
This is YOUR to-do list- not theirs.

RELATIONSHIP

Full Moon

Release the past. Do a Fire Ceremony that represents the history of your relationship. Write the significant moments and experiences of your relationship on a paper. Give it to the flames and let it go. This clears and cleanses the energy for your relationship to be fresh and new.

Notes

Placing Selenite Crystals under your bed supports in clearing energy in your room and keeping your bed a place where energy is balanced.

Dream Work Process:
The moon is in the realm of subconscious as it pulls on the energy and emotions we often carry unaware.

Before you go to sleep, place a crystal beneath your pillow. Clear quartz or amethyst are great for your intuition.

Say outloud: "I ask that my higher self and inner knowing teach me while I sleep. Send me the truth that I am ready to know."

Record your dreams or feelings in the morning in a dream journal. Don't over think. Sometimes the message doesn't make sense at the time- but does looking back.

This process is especially powerful during Full Moons.

Wolf Moon January:

Wolf Moon is a time to gather with your pack. Who is your inner circle? Who do you trust? Who do you connect with? Are you putting the most important people in your life at the top of your list? Do your most important relationships take precedence over other obligations? This is a time for prioritizing and protecting your den. As you see your inner circle, ask if they are living in a way you would choose to live for your greatest life. Scientific studies show that we are who we spend the most time with. Reflect now about who you want to be like: energetically, relationships, financially, spiritually, ethically, etc. Do the people you spend the most time with and put the most energy into- reflect these ideals? Wolf moon is also about the HOWL. Crying out, speaking your truth. Declaring your claim of worthiness in the universal flow. Be courageous. Be open. Speak your truth.

Full Moon Notes
I am grateful for... I now release...

New Moon Notes
I now create and gracefully receive...

Snow Moon February:
Snow moon is the last moon of winter. It is the end of the cold and the darkness. It is the edge of our limitations. We are moving out of the tunnel. What have you learned about the shadows in you? How did you overcome them? As the snow falls it is a time for self-reflection. Have you grown, have you learned? What did the long winter teach you? It is often our hardships and struggles that cause us to grow. Here, at the end of the long winter- did you store away enough sustenance to make it through? Historically, we had to work all year to creating food stores to survive- but in modern day our challenges are often energetic and emotional.

How are you filling your "stores" to sustain you in the dark and cold times? It is UP TO YOU.

Full Moon Notes
I am grateful for... I now release...

New Moon Notes
I now create and gracefully receive...

Worm/Crow Moon March:
This is the softening of the soil. The Earthworms begin to rise up out of the darkness and search for food. The Earthworm represents survival and ingenuity. They can change direction and move wherever they are led to go. Even in the circumstance of tragedy and pain (being cut in half) they will survive and use their ingenuity. Crows are intuitive and intelligent. They are cunning and attracted to shiny things. Don't let illusions catch your eye, focus on real wealth and dreams.

Equinox

Full Moon Notes
I am grateful for... I now release...

New Moon Notes
I now create and gracefully receive...

Spring Equinox Notes

How is my life balanced for this next year to be the best yet?

Home, Family, Spirit, Health, Finance, Career, Self-Growth?

Notes

Pink Moon April:
The light is soft and beautiful. The shadows are disappearing. It is time to start implementing the plans, preparation, and the wisdom you have spent the winter months doing. There is warmth coming. Light is expanding. Plant your gardens.

Full Moon Notes
I am grateful for... I now release...

New Moon Notes
I now create and gracefully receive...

Flower Moon May:
The buds are beginning to show. There is beauty and fragrance and music. The flowers are hope. They exist to be nothing more or less than they are. Flowers are "Heaven" energy. Heaven on Earth. Flowers are the embodiment of BEING, while GROWING. Perfect as a tiny bud, and in full bloom. REMEMBER to be patient with yourself. BE. Know you are always expanding, and you are perfect right where you are.

Every flower is perfect.
So are you.

Full Moon Notes
I am grateful for... I now release...

New Moon Notes
I now create and gracefully receive...

Strawberry/Rose Moon June:
The fruits of your labors are manifesting. Now is not the time to quit. The seed needs cultivation in order to grow. This is the time when we start to get bored; we are seeing results and the temptation to relax a little and get lazy a little comes in. Stay connected and cultivating. Yes, it's a little easier now, stay disciplined, stay in your heart, keep moving forward.

Stay dedicated to your future and priorities. Balance work, family, spirit, fun, and creation.

What are some ways to stay motivated?

What is a habit you can implement to keep you focused?

Summer Solstice
June 21-22

Full Moon Notes
I am grateful for... I now release...

New Moon Notes
I now create and gracefully receive...

Buck/Thunder Moon July:
There are storms that will come. Remember to rise above the storms. Remember that as the water falls and sometimes all seems lost, it is just a rearranging of nutrients. Watch the majesty of nature and her beauty. Be one with it. KNOW that you are not separate from it, but you are it.

What are some storms you have faced or are facing?
How have they or are they making you stronger?
What is the bigger purpose of the storms in your life?

The Buck is the Totem animal of personal sovereignty and humble nobility.
Remember who you are and that you have a personal path - no matter how deep or thick the forest

Full Moon Notes
I am grateful for... I now release...

New Moon Notes
I now create and gracefully receive...

Sturgeon/Red Moon August:
The fall is approaching. The light is beautiful and languid and revitalizing. What do you love? What brings you your greatest joy and passion? What do you dream of? How are you living your dreams now? What changes have you seen from the beginning of the year?

Sturgeon reminds us to flow with the river of life. Our passions and interests are what lead us to our divine purpose.

Full Moon Notes
I am grateful for... I now release...

New Moon Notes
I now create and gracefully receive...

Harvest Moon September:
Harvest Moon is a time for receiving. It is a time to end a cycle to celebrate your achievements for the year and to take inventory of where you are. What would you do differently? What worked out this year? What didn't? This is a time for honest reflection and awareness. This is a time to be grateful and to celebrate your accomplishments. Often, we set goals and achieve them without acknowledging their completion. When we do this, we rob ourselves of the satisfaction of our growth and acceptance- which perpetuates a cycle that "enough is never enough." CELEBRATE, Feast, write a list of your successes. Make a toast to you.

Equinox

Full Moon Notes
I am grateful for... I now release...

New Moon Notes
I now create and gracefully receive...

Fall Equinox Notes

Is my life in balance?

How has this year changed my priorities?

Family, Health, Home, Relationships, Finance, Career, Self-Growth?

Notes

Hunter's Moon October:
Set your targets and goals. Traditionally, the Hunter's Moon means it's time to gather meat and pelts for the cold months. This moon is about focus. Setting your goals for next year. Hunting takes preparation, skill, practice, sharpening spears and arrows. The winter months were used to prepare and repair tools and weapons, to track, to refine skills. As you've taken inventory (Harvest Moon) it's time to consider the next focus and goal for next year's moons. What is the target?

Where do you need to sharpen your skills?

Full Moon Notes
I am grateful for... I now release...

New Moon Notes
I now create and gracefully receive...

Beaver Moon November:
Beavers prepare their dens to survive the dark and cold months. This is the period of building your foundation. Take classes, read, research, study, invest in your important relationships. With the natural season of snow and winter- stay closer to home; meaning- don't try to go in all different directions. It is the time and season to work on the den. To fortify YOU.

Full Moon Notes
I am grateful for... I now release...

New Moon Notes
I now create and gracefully receive...

Cold Moon December:
This moon coincides with Winter Solstice. It is time to self-care. It is time to know who you are in the dark. To declare your light during darkest times. To learn to light the fire within and learn to sustain your own light and life. This is a time of sitting by the fire and reflecting and learning the soothe of your own soul's rhythm.

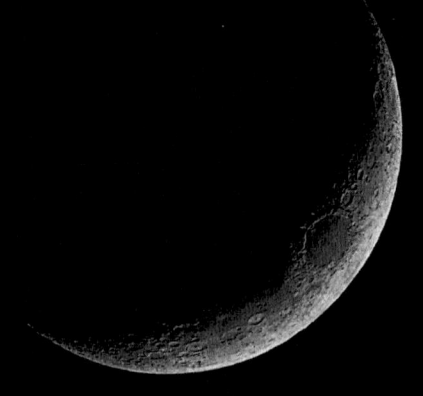

Winter Solstice
December 21-22

Full Moon Notes
I am grateful for... I now release...

New Moon Notes
I now create and gracefully receive...

Notes

The Parent I choose to be:

We have the choice every day to be our best.
Parenthood is challenging and easy to
take for granted in our every day routine.
Secret: Parenting is for us.
Yes, we do it for our kids- but parenting is about
the type of person we are.
Nothing refines us like being a Mother or
Father- and guess what?
You can do it YOUR way.

Notes

The Moon is the
Reflection.
How is my life reflecting
my inner self?

The Moon creates no light of its own.
It captures our rapture by its ability
to reflect the light it's given.

What are you creating in your life?
How is your hidden subconscious
influencing your life that you
may not realize?

Notes

Do I Trust Me?

If I treated my friend the way I treat myself-
would we still be friends?
Do I keep promises to myself?
Do I keep my focus on my goals?
Do I say kind things to me?

Create NEW patterns of self-talk.
Release OLD patterns self-talk.

I KNOW
My Strength

What is something you never thought you could have done... but did it?

What are you overcoming?

The dream I let go of.
Do I choose to reawaken?

Dreams not followed
haunt us like shadows.

What dream did you give up?

Why?

If money and time weren't an issue...

What would that dream look like?

Notes

I choose to create a new reality: My dreams are possible.

Write a story. Make it simple. One or two pages.
Use your life as inspiration, but make it fictional.
With YOUR beginning, but whatever ending you choose.
Make it fun.

Notes

Notes

Where I sabotage my light...
I now release.

Notes

My Scars Don't Define me

Physically and emotionally, we have scars.

We can still have an amazing life.

Notes

Notes

The Growth I Am Experiencing

The Horizon
My Dreams and Goals

What is my 5-year life vision?

Notes

While I sleep,
My Soul is ever awake.

Guide my dreams:

Notes

Every mountain top is breached with one step at a time.

Don't get overwhelmed by the height of the mountain- just keep going. Take the next step.

What is your next step?

Notes

My New Prosperity Beginning Today is:

Notes

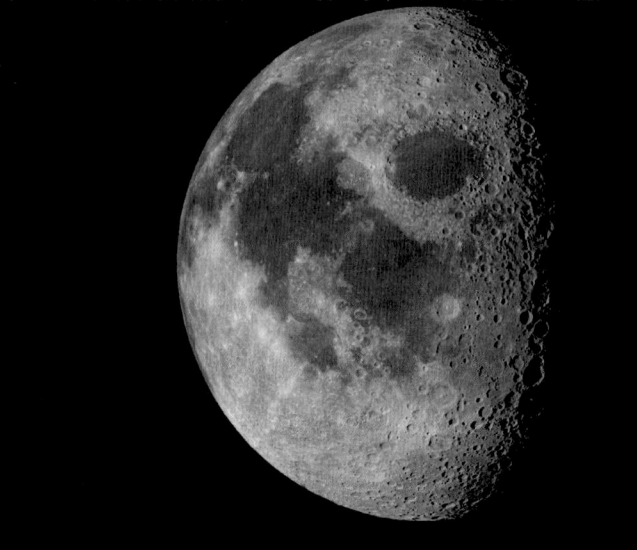

Where I am learning Balance

Notes